Properties of Materials

Floating or Sinking

Charlotte Guillain

Heinemann Library
Chicago, Illinois

www.heinemannraintree.com
Visit our website to find out
more information about
Heinemann-Raintree books.

To order:
☎ Phone 888-454-2279
💻 Visit www.heinemannraintree.com
  to browse our catalog and order online.

Designed by Joanna Hinton-Malivoire
Photo research by Elizabeth Alexander
Printed and bound by South China Printing Company Ltd

13 12 11 10 09
10 9 8 7 6 5 4 3 2 1

Library of Congress Cataloging-in-Publication Data
Guillain, Charlotte.
  Floating or sinking / Charlotte Guillain.
    p. cm. -- (Properties of materials)
  Includes bibliographical references and index.
  ISBN 978-1-4329-3290-9 (hc) -- ISBN 978-1-4329-3298-5
(pb) 1. Floating bodies--Juvenile literature. 2. Buoyant ascent
(Hydrodynamics)--Juvenile literature. 3. Hydrostatics--Juvenile
literature. I. Title.
  QC147.5.G85 2008
  532'.25--dc22
                                    2008055126

Acknowledgments
The author and publishers are grateful to the following for
permission to reproduce copyright material: Alamy p. **17** (©
81A); © Capstone Publishers pp. **7**, **18**, **19**, **22** (Karon Dubke);
Corbis pp. **5** (© Jose Fuste Raga), **6** (© Andy Newman/epa),
12 (© Frans Lanting); Getty Images pp. **10** (AFP/Stringer),
15 (Gulfimages), **16** (Richard Elliott/Photographer's Choice);
Photolibrary pp. **4** (Ben Davidson/Animals Animals), **8**, **23 top**
(81A Productions), **11**, **23 middle** (Mirko Zanni/WaterFrame –
Underwater Images), **13** (Wolfgang Herath/imagebroker.net), **21**
(J.W. Alker/imagebroker.net); Shutterstock pp. **9** (© mangojuicy),
14 (© Max Blain), **20**, **23** bottom (© newphotoservice).

Cover photograph of river rafting reproduced with permission
of Shutterstock (© Jörg Jahn). Back cover photograph of a stone
sinking in water reproduced with permission of Photolibrary
(81A Productions).

The publishers would like to thank Nancy Harris and Adriana
Scalise for their assistance in the preparation of this book.

Every effort has been made to contact copyright holders
of any material reproduced in this book. Any omissions will
be rectified in subsequent printings if notice is given to
the publisher.

Contents

Materials That Float

Some things can float.

Things that float can be flat.

Things that float can be heavy.

Things that float can be light.

Materials That Sink

Some things can sink.

Things that sink can be light.

Things that sink can be heavy.

Things that sink can be solid.

Materials That Float or Sink

Wood can float.

Wood can sink.

Metal can float.

Metal can sink.

Paper can float.

Paper can sink.

Glass can float.

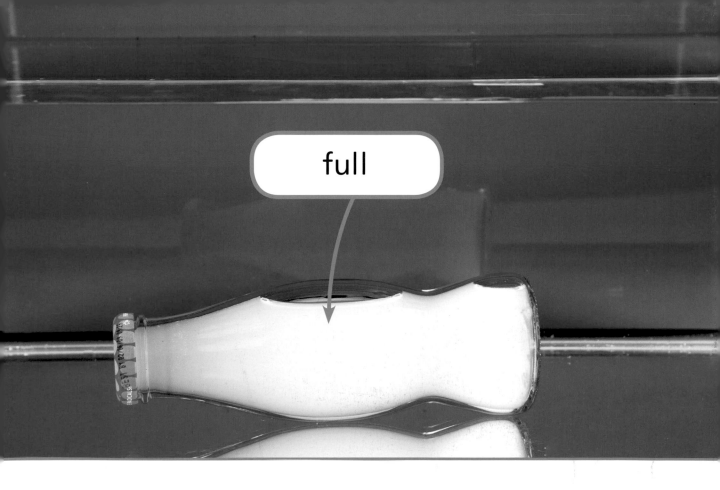

Glass can sink.

surface

Things that float stay on top of the water.

Things that sink go to the bottom of
the water.

Quiz

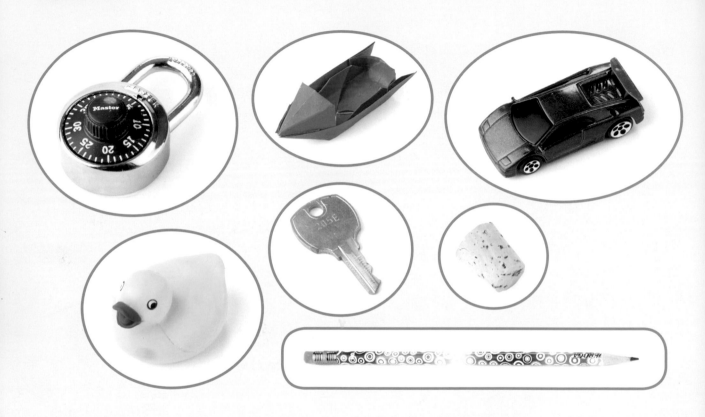

Which of these things float?

Which of these things sink?

Picture Glossary

sink drop below the surface of water and move down toward the bottom

solid fixed shape that is not a gas or a liquid

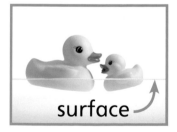

surface

surface top part of something

Index

Note to Parents and Teachers
Before Reading
Explain to children that materials that float stay on top of water. Materials that sink go to the bottom of water. Have children describe things they have seen sink or float.

After Reading
Give groups of children a bucket of water and a bag of different materials (e.g., rock, a foil cup, a square of paper, a straw, a foam ball, a penny, bathtub toys, and wooden blocks). Place children in groups. Tell children to make predictions and record whether each object will sink or float in water. Children can record their predictions on a pre-made worksheet or in a journal. As children place their objects in the water, have them observe what happens. After children are done exploring sinking and floating objects, ask the children the following questions:
1. How many of your predictions were correct?
2. Describe the objects that sank. What do they have in common?
3. Describe the objects that floated. What do they have in common?